WHERE DO I LIVE?

TOWN

A Crabtree Roots Book

ALICIA RODRIGUEZ

Crabtree Publishing
crabtreebooks.com

School-to-Home Support for Caregivers and Teachers

This book helps children grow by letting them practice reading. Here are a few guiding questions to help the reader with building his or her comprehension skills. Possible answers appear here in red.

Before Reading:

- What do I think this book is about?
    - *I think this book is about towns.*
    - *I think this book is about what we can find in a town.*
- What do I want to learn about this topic?
    - *I want to learn how big a town is.*
    - *I want to learn what a town looks like.*

During Reading:

- I wonder why...
    - *I wonder what makes a town different from a city.*
    - *I wonder why a town has its own government.*
- What have I learned so far?
    - *I have learned that a mayor is the leader of a town.*
    - *I have learned that a town can have houses, schools, and stores.*

After Reading:

- What details did I learn about this topic?
    - *I have learned that most towns have a Town Hall.*
    - *I have learned that most towns have a small number of people living there.*
- Read the book again and look for the vocabulary words.
    - *I see the word **street** on page 4 and the word **mayor** on page 6. The other vocabulary words are found on page 14.*

I live in a **town**.

There is a main **street**

It has many **shops**.

The **mayor** is the leader.

He works at **Town Hall**.

My school is in my town.

There is a **fire station**, too.

18 SQUAD CO. 18
SQUAD 18
N.Y.

I enjoy my town.

NO TURN ON RED
IRONVILLE UMC

Word List

Sight Words

a
at
has
he
I
in
is
it
live
my
the
there
too
works

Words to Know

fire station

mayor

shops

street

town

Town Hall

40 Words

I live in a **town**.

There is a main **street**.

It has many **shops**.

The **mayor** is the leader.

He works at the **Town Hall**.

My school is in my town.

There is a **fire station**, too.

I enjoy my town.

WHERE DO I LIVE?
TOWN

Written by: Alicia Rodriguez
Designed by: Rhea Wallace
Series Development: James Earley
Proofreader: Janine Deschenes
Educational Consultant: Marie Lemke M.Ed.
Production manager: Candice Campbell

Photographs:
Shutterstock: Roberto Galan: cover; George Sheldon; p. 1; Sean Pavone: p. 3, 14; Marekuliasz: p. 4-5, 14; Page Light Studios: p. 6, 8, 14; Bob LoCicero; p. 7, 14; JJFara: p. 11, 14

Crabtree Publishing

crabtreebooks.com 800-387-7650

In Canada: We acknowledge the financial support of the Government of Canada through the Canada Book Fund for our publishing activities.

Printed in the U.S.A./CP022026

Published in Canada
Crabtree Publishing
616 Welland Avenue
St. Catharines, Ontario
L2M 5V6

Published in the United States
Crabtree Publishing
347 Fifth Avenue
Suite 1402-145
New York, NY 10016

Hardcover	978-1-4271-6003-4
Paperback	978-1-4271-6009-6
Ebook (pdf)	978-1-4271-3362-5
Epub	978-1-4271-3422-6
Read-along	978-1-4271-6027-0
Audio book	978-1-4271-6033-1

Library and Archives Canada Cataloguing in Publication

Title: Town / Alicia Rodriguez.
Names: Rodriguez, Alicia (Children's author), author.
Description: Series statement: Where do I live? | "A Crabtree roots book".
Identifiers: Canadiana (print) 2021018289X | Canadiana (ebook) 20210182903 | ISBN 9781427160034 (hardcover) | ISBN 9781427160096 (softcover) | ISBN 9781427133625 (HTML) | ISBN 9781427134226 (EPUB) | ISBN 9781427160270 (read-along ebook)
Subjects: LCSH: City and town life—Juvenile literature.
Classification: LCC HT152 .R64 2022 | DDC j307.76/3—dc23

Library of Congress Cataloging-in-Publication Data

Names: Rodriguez, Alicia (Children's author), author.
Title: Town / Alicia Rodriguez.
Other titles: At head of title: Where do I live?
Description: New York, NY : Crabtree Publishing Company, [2022 | Series: Where do I live? A Crabtree roots book | Includes index.
Identifiers: LCCN 2021015138 (print) | LCCN 2021015139 (ebook) | ISBN 9781427160034 (hardcover) | ISBN 9781427160096 (paperback) | ISBN 9781427133625 (ebook) | ISBN 9781427134226 (epub) | ISBN 9781427160270
Subjects: LCSH: Cities and towns--Juvenile literature.
Classification: LCC HT152 .R6339 2022 (print) | LCC HT152 (ebook) | DDC 307.76--dc23
LC record available at https://lccn.loc.gov/2021015138
LC ebook record available at https://lccn.loc.gov/2021015139